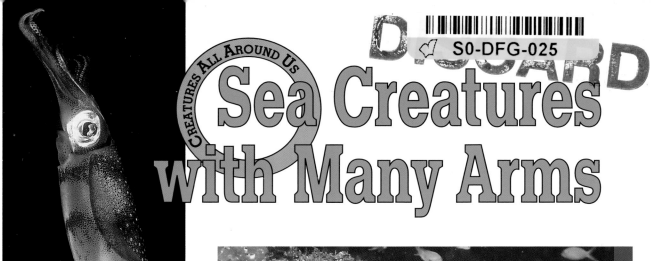

Sea Creatures with Many Arms

CREATURES ALL AROUND US

by D. M. Souza

🌿 Carolrhoda Books, Inc./Minneapolis

The publisher wishes to thank Janet Voight, PhD, of the Department of Zoology at the Field Museum of Natural History in Chicago, for her help in the preparation of this book.

Carolrhoda Books, Inc. c/o The Lerner Publishing Group
241 First Avenue North, Minneapolis, MN 55401 U.S.A.

Website address: www.lernerbooks.com

Library of Congress Cataloging-in-Publication Data

Souza, D. M. (Dorothy M.)
    Sea creatures with many arms / by D. M. Souza
      p.   cm. – (Creatures all around us)
    Includes index.
    Summary: Describes the physical characteristics, behavior, habitat, and life cycle of cephalopods.
    ISBN 1-57505-262-8
    1. Cephalopoda—Juvenile literature. [1. Cephalopods.]
I. Title. II. Series: Souza, D. M. (Dorothy M.). Creatures all around us.
    QL430.2.S6   1998
    594'.5—dc21   97-17997

Sea Creatures with Many Arms

A twin-spotted octopus changes color to blend into the rocky ocean floor.

An orange-colored creature creeps slowly along the ocean floor on arms longer than its body. Suddenly, a large fish appears from out of the shadows. To hide, the creature pulls its arms in close and presses its round body against the sand. Its color changes from orange to tan, to match the color of the sand. The fish does not see the creature and swims away.

The chambered nautilus (top) may have as many as ninety arms. The cuttlefish (bottom) shoots out its two tentacles to catch a meal.

Meet the octopus, a cephalopod (SEH-fuh-luh-pod), or animal with many arms around its head. The squid, cuttlefish, and chambered nautilus—relatives of the octopus—are also cephalopods.

How many arms do cephalopods have? The octopus, squid, and cuttlefish each have eight. The chambered nautilus may have as many as ninety. Squid and cuttlefish also have two **tentacles**, longer arms that they use to grab food. When not hunting, a squid usually folds back its tentacles. The cuttlefish hides them in pouches found near its eyes. But if the squid or cuttlefish spot **prey**, or the animals they like to eat, their tentacles shoot out to nab the meal.

On the underside of most cephalopods' arms are rows of suckers, or sticky suction cups, which the animals use to hold onto food. Some octopuses have as many as 240 suckers on each arm.

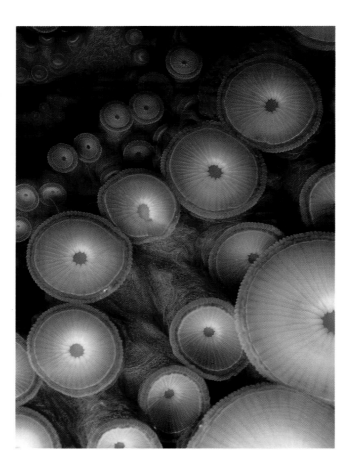

The octopus has hundreds of suckers on each of its arms to help it crawl over rocks and grab onto food.

Mollusks, like this pond snail, are soft-bodied animals without backbones.

All cephalopods belong to a larger group of animals known as mollusks (MAH-lusks), soft-bodied creatures without backbones. While mollusks such as clams, oysters, and snails are covered by shells, most cephalopods are not. The chambered nautilus is the only cephalopod that lives inside a shell.

Like other mollusks, cephalopods have a **mantle,** or layer of skin, covering most of their bodies. Beneath the mantle are the animals' organs and a hollow space known as the **mantle cavity.** This cavity holds a pair of gills, feathery organs that help the animals breathe. Water enters the mantle cavity through a slit on the animal's underside. Then it passes over the gills. The gills take air from the water. Then muscles pump the water out through a funnel, which is a tubelike opening to the outside.

The octopus's mantle covers its organs.

Octopuses are, perhaps, the smartest of all cephalopods. This octopus is learning to travel through a maze that was set up by scientists.

Cephalopods have the largest brains of any animal without a backbone. Some scientists who work with octopuses in laboratories believe octopuses are the smartest of all cephalopods. Octopuses can be taught to slither through mazes, recognize different shapes, and unscrew lids of jars containing crabs.

About 700 species (SPEE-sheez), or kinds, of cephalopods have been discovered in salty waters around the world. Some are smaller than your little finger. Others are as long as a school bus. Many can change colors in seconds and make their skin as smooth as jelly or as uneven as goosebumps. Most of these creatures can also squirt ink and zip through the water. Let's watch a few in action and discover how and why they do what they do.

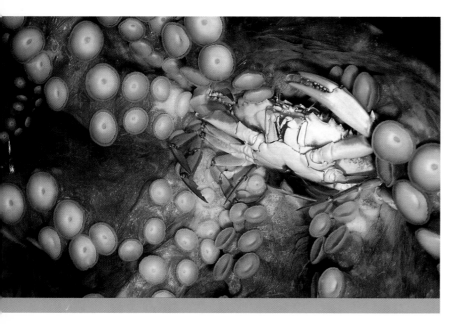

Tricks and Treats

An octopus uses its suckers to bring a crab to its mouth for a tasty meal.

Several rocks form a small, dark cave on the ocean floor. A plump crab crawls slowly past the opening. From inside the cave, the large, bulging eyes of an octopus peer out.

One of the octopus's 3-foot-long arms snakes toward the crab. It grips the wiggling body with several suckers and brings the crab to its sharp, bony beak. (The octopus has a beak like a parrot's—its lower jaw sticks out in front of its upper one.)

10

Holding the crab tightly, the octopus jabs its beak into the shell, flooding its prey with poison from a special structure called a gland inside its mouth. In minutes, the crab is paralyzed, or unable to move. The poison also softens the crab's flesh to almost a liquid, making it easy for the octopus to suck the flesh out of the shell. After finishing its meal, the animal tosses away the shell and waits for another treat to pass by its rocky den.

All cephalopods are carnivores (KAR-nuh-vorz), or meat eaters. Their favorite foods are crabs, lobsters, shrimp, and fish. In a single night, a 50-pound octopus can eat twenty or more crabs or lobsters, a meal that weighs almost as much as the octopus does.

Lobsters, like this American lobster, are yummy treats for cephalopods.

In warm waters off the coast of Australia, a cuttlefish with two huge, black eyes searches the seafloor for food. The upper part of its flat body is covered with zebralike stripes that range in color from brown to violet. On its belly are bluish green spots. Two fins, used for swimming, extend the length of its mantle.

This cuttlefish uses its fins to swim or float in the water. Zebralike stripes decorate its mantle, and spots cover its belly.

This common cuttlefish enjoys a delicious meal.

The cuttlefish spots a crab crawling nearby. In a flash, it moves behind its prey, whips out two tentacles with club-shaped ends, grabs the crab, and pulls the meal to its mouth. With several of its arms holding the crab in place, the cuttlefish uses its beak to bite into the shell. Then it scoops out the crab's flesh with its **radula** (RAH-juh-luh), or tooth-lined tongue.

While most cephalopods hunt alone, as the octopus and cuttlefish do, many squid search for food in schools, or large groups. Common squid gather at night near the surface of the ocean. Their rocket-shaped bodies move together. As soon as a school of herring, their favorite food, appears, the squid quickly circle the fish. Each squid reaches out with its two tentacles, grabs a fish, and brings the meal to its mouth. With powerful jaws, the squid tears the herring into pieces while its toothy tongue shoves the food down its throat. Then the school of squid moves on, looking for more fish to catch.

These squid have gathered together to hunt for food.

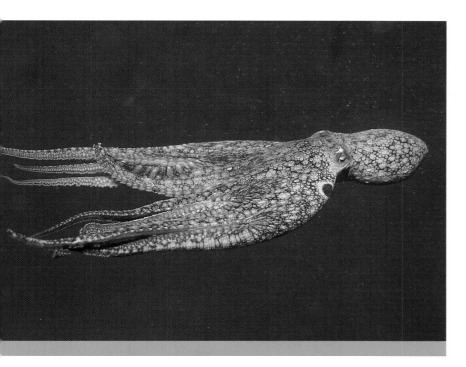

Jet Power

An octopus zips through the water.

You know what happens when you fill a balloon with air and let it go before tying its open end—the balloon zips away like a jet plane. Many cephalopods move through the sea in a similar way. They take extra water into their mantle cavity. Then muscles squeeze the water out through the funnel. This makes cephalopods jet through the sea the way a balloon zips through the air.

The cephalopod with the most jet power is the squid. Fins on each side of its body help it to turn quickly even while moving fast. Squid are able to burst ahead at speeds of up to 3 or 4 miles an hour. But they cannot do this for any great distance. A few kinds of squid use their jet power to shoot themselves out of the water when they're being chased. Some have jumped as high as 50 feet and landed on the decks of ships.

The squid is the fastest of all cephalopods. It can travel 3 or 4 miles an hour for short spurts. During this time, its fins help the squid to turn quickly.

The cuttlefish spends most of its time floating in the water with its arms hanging down.

Next to the squid, the cuttlefish is a slowpoke. It often floats in one place, wiggling its skirtlike fins and letting its arms hang like seaweed. To move up or down, the animal uses a small soft shell called a **cuttlebone** found inside its body. The cuttlebone feels like chalk and contains many empty spaces. When the cuttlefish fills the empty spaces with water, its body becomes heavier and settles to the bottom. When the creature releases the water, the spaces fill with air, and the cuttlefish floats toward the surface. If an enemy comes near, however, the cuttlefish will use its jet power to make a fast getaway.

Like a cuttlefish, an octopus jets away when it feels threatened. Most of the time, though, it travels by crawling. With its suckers, it grabs onto rocks and pulls itself forward. Some deep-sea varieties of octopus swim by gracefully waving the webs of skin that connect one arm to the next. A few have webs that reach almost to the tips of their arms. When these creatures swim, they look like umbrellas opening and closing.

An octopus crawls across a coral reef.

Danger!

The moray eel likes to eat octopuses.

Crawling slowly toward its rocky den, an octopus spots a moray eel, a fish that likes to eat octopuses. Quickly the octopus flattens and squeezes its boneless body through a narrow opening between two rocks. Since the eel cannot fit through the opening, it swims around looking for another way to catch its prey. Meanwhile, the octopus slips out of its hideout and jets away. The moray eel spots it and follows close behind.

To keep enemies from spotting it, a common octopus squirts ink into the water and then zips away to safety.

This time, the octopus squirts a cloud of purple liquid through its funnel. The ink muddies the water and makes it hard for the eel to see. While its enemy snaps at the dark cloud, the octopus escapes.

Many cephalopods squirt ink to escape **predators** (PREH-duh-turz), or animals that hunt them. Some squid even squirt a liquid that can give off light. As the liquid mixes with the water, it shines with tiny points of gray-green light. Since these lights look like hundreds of moving creatures, predators become confused.

To keep from being spotted by enemies, cephalopods often camouflage (KAM-uh-flazh) themselves, or make themselves blend in with their surroundings. An octopus crawling over coral can turn whatever color the coral is—rose, white, peach, or some other color.

This octopus has started to change color to match its surroundings.

The master of camouflage is the cuttlefish. Not only can it turn different colors, it can make itself look as if it's covered with spots, stripes, and zigzag lines. Like other cephalopods, the cuttlefish has millions of organs under its skin called **chromatophores** (kroh-MA-tuh-forz). These are pinpoint-size packets of **pigments,** or colors, that can change shape when the animal's brain sends them a signal.

When a cuttlefish, for example, is frightened or excited, tiny muscles pull the packets sideways, making different colors spread out over the surface of the animal's body. The colors can even take the shape of spots, stripes, or zigzag lines. As the muscles relax, the chromatophores become small again, and the colors seem to disappear. All this can happen in less than a second.

This cuttlefish changes the pattern on its body to blend in with the coral.

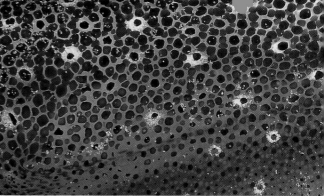

To confuse its predators, these squid (left) light up—there are even lights around their eyes! Tiny lights on this squid (above) cover its body—including its fins.

A number of cephalopods also have special organs called **photophores** (FO-tuh-forz), which light up. Some squid have them around their eyes, and on their arms, head, and body. Others have them only around one eye. One squid was found with two hundred lights on its body!

Camouflage not only confuses predators such as whales, seals, and fish—it also helps cephalopods find mates. They often use ink, color changes, and twinkling lights to let each other know it's time to raise a family.

Millions of Eggs

The male cuttlefish may turn pale yellow when it's ready to find a mate.

When male cephalopods are ready to mate, they do unusual things. A cuttlefish may turn pale yellow and show off purplish-brown stripes. Squid and octopuses often shimmer with color to attract the attention of females. A squid may dance face-to-face with a female for a few seconds and then wrap his arms around hers.

Many male cephalopods have a special arm, called the **hectocotylus** (HEK-teh-KAHT-luhs), which they use when mating. A male octopus, for example, will approach a female by stroking her with this arm. Next, he uses the arm to place a tube of sperm, called a **spermatophore** (spur-MAT-uh-for), in an opening near her funnel. As soon as they are released, the sperm join with the female's eggs and fertilize (FUR-tul-eyz) them, or make them develop into young.

Two male octopuses mate with a female. The males extend sperm-filled arms toward the female to deposit a tube of sperm inside of her.

Female cephalopods lay their eggs in a variety of places. The common cuttlefish releases as many as 500 eggs, one at a time, and attaches them to a rock or the branches of an underwater plant. The brown or black eggs, colored by her ink, look like bunches of small grapes. In about four months, inch-long cuttlefish break out of their eggs and begin to swim.

These cuttlefish mate on a coral reef. After mating, the female will release her eggs and attach them to a nearby rock.

This female squid releases a fingerlike capsule that contains eggs.

Female common squid lay between 10 and 20 fingerlike capsules. Each capsule contains about 100 eggs. The female attaches the capsules to rocks or other hard objects on the floor of the sea. After about 30 days, baby squid begin to break out of their egg cases. They are smaller than the nail on your little finger.

Neither cuttlefish nor squid watch over their eggs once they are laid. The parents die soon after mating and egg laying. The female common octopus never leaves her eggs, however. Each egg is white, slightly oval, and smaller than a single grain of rice. The octopus attaches thousands of them to thin strings, hanging them from the ceiling of her den like shiny decorations.

Thousands of octopus eggs, each smaller than a grain of rice, hang in strings from the ceiling of a female octopus's den.

The female octopus takes great care to keep her eggs clean and safe. Until the eggs hatch, the female will not leave them.

To keep her eggs clean, the female showers them daily with water from her funnel. Then she wipes them with her suction cups. If a predator approaches, she shields the eggs with upturned arms and defends them even if her own life is threatened. She does not take any time out for herself—not even to eat.

Some octopuses break out of their cases sooner than others. Those that are still developing will soon hatch and leave the den.

As the embryos (EM-bree-ohz), or developing babies, grow inside a clear covering, their eyes, color sacs, and ink sacs begin to take shape. Soon the tiny creatures can see out just as well as their mother can see in.

After about 40 days, tiny bubblelike bodies with eight arms break out of the clear coverings and begin to float around. But not all the eggs hatch at once. The mother octopus continues to guard, wash, and wipe the slower ones for about a week. By the time the last ones leave the den, their mother is so weak from lack of food that she soon dies. But her young float through the water, squirting clouds of ink at creatures that try to eat them.

After hatching, the baby octopuses leave the safety of their mother's den. This tiny octopus is ready to find its own food and defend itself from enemies.

Shells
with Rooms

The chambered nautilus makes a shell to cover its body.

An unusual cephalopod lives about 900 to 1500 feet beneath the warm waters near many South Pacific islands. If you saw its coiled shell, you might think it was a giant snail. But the creature is a chambered nautilus, the only cephalopod that makes a shell to cover its body.

The chambered nautilus's body is only a few inches long, but its smooth, lightweight shell may measure up to 10 inches across. Millions of years ago, some of its relatives had shells 15 feet across.

As a chambered nautilus grows, it does an amazing thing. It builds a larger chamber, or room, next to its old one until it has a giant curved house with many rooms. Each empty room is then sealed off with a thin wall known as a **septum.** Some adult chambered nautiluses have as many as 27 to 30 chambers inside their shells. But they always live in the one closest to the outside.

When it outgrows its old room, this chambered nautilus will make a new, larger room to live in.

Even though it has a pair of large eyes, the chambered nautilus does not see well in the dark parts of the ocean where it lives. This creature must depend more on smell and touch to discover its surroundings.

If it senses a predator nosing in too close, the chambered nautilus closes the entrance of its shell with a leathery piece of red-and-white skin known as the **hood.** When the animal wants to see if its enemy has gone, it either lifts the hood partway or pulls it back over its head.

To hide from predators, the chambered nautilus pulls a red-and-white hood over itself for protection.

This chambered nautilus has found a dead fish to eat.

During the day, a chambered nautilus often rests deep in the sea. At night it moves closer to the surface to search for tiny shrimp or pieces of dead fish to eat. As soon as it feels or smells food, the tip of one of its many arms reaches out and grabs the food, not with suckers, but with a sticky fold of skin. The chambered nautilus's radula tears the food apart and carries it into the stomach.

Hovering off a coral wall, a chambered nautilus floats in the water.

Although the chambered nautilus can jet frontwards, backwards, and sideways, most of the time it just drifts up and down in the water. It cannot shoot out a cloud of ink or change colors, as other cephalopods can. But somehow this slow-moving creature has survived for millions of years. The chambered nautilus gives us some idea of how other cephalopods with shells on their backs once lived in the oceans.

Scientists still have much to learn about cephalopods. Is the octopus really the smartest of them all? How do giant squid live in the deep parts of the ocean? Are other strange cephalopods hiding in the seas?

As scientists continue their studies and explore parts of the oceans where few people have ever gone before, they will, no doubt, find answers to these and other questions about cephalopods. We can only imagine what future generations will be saying about these amazing creatures with many arms.

Scientists continue to find new facts about the octopus and other cephalopods as they explore the oceans.

About 700 different kinds of cephalopods can be found in salty waters around the world. All have soft bodies and many arms surrounding their head. Some are less than an inch long, while others are the size of giants. Below are a few facts about some members of this unusual class of sea creatures.

CEPHALOPOD	SIZE	FAVORITE FOODS	WHERE FOUND	ENEMIES
Chambered nautilus	3-9 inches	small fish, shellfish	coral reefs in warm waters near many South Pacific islands	stormy seas that wash them ashore, humans
Common octopus	3-10 feet	shellfish	coastal waters around the world	moray eels
Common squid	7-20 inches	small fish	in waters around the world, near surface, especially at night	sharks, large fish, humans
Cuttlefish	3 inches-5½ feet	shrimp	tropical waters near seafloor	dolphins
Giant octopus	20-32 feet	shellfish, rockfish, flatfish	deep seas from northern Asia to Alaska and California	sea otters, seals
Giant squid	25-55 feet	fish	deep waters, open sea around the world	whales

Glossary

chromatophores: organs under the skin of some animals that help them change colors

cuttlebone: the soft, chalky shell inside the body of a cuttlefish

hectocotylus: a special arm some male cephalopods use in mating

hood: a leathery piece of skin that closes the entrance of a chambered nautilus's shell

mantle: a layer of skin covering most of a mollusk's body

mantle cavity: a water-filled space within a mollusk's body

photophores: organs that light up on the bodies of some animals such as squid

pigments: the colorings found under the skin of some cephalopods

predators: animals that hunt and eat other animals

prey: an animal that is killed and eaten by other animals

radula: the tooth-lined tongue of many mollusks

septum: a wall dividing the rooms of a chambered nautilus

spermatophore: a tube of sperm, or male cells, that the male cephalopod places inside the female to fertilize her eggs

tentacles: the two longest arms of squid and cuttlefish that are used for grabbing food

Index

The photographs are reproduced through the courtesy of: © Norbert Wu, front cover, pp. 8, 15, 17, 24, 25, 26, 27, 30, 31, 36; © Hal Beral/Visuals Unlimited, back cover; Tom Stack & Associates: (© Dave B. Fleetham) pp. 1 (left), 5 (top), 37, (© Larry Tackett) pp. 1 (right), 18, (© Randy Morse) pp. 6, 21, 23 (right), (© Gary Milburn) p. 10, (© Mike Severns) p. 16, (© Ed Robinson) p. 20; The National Audubon Society Collection/Photo Researchers: (© Gregory Ochocki) p. 3, (© R. J. Erwin) p. 7, (© Andrew J. Martinez) pp. 11, 19, (© Mike Neumann) p. 22, (© Tom McHugh) pp. 28, 32, 33, (© Douglas Faulkner) pp. 34, 35; Root Resources/© Lynn Funkhouser, p. 5 (bottom); © Roger Hanlon/Visuals Unlimited, p. 9; Animals Animals: (© Miriam Austerman) p. 12, (© G. I. Bernard) p. 13; © Bob Cranston/Mo Yung Productions, pp. 14, 23 (left), 29.